Pandemic!
The Delirious Variant

Stories, poems, and thoughts written during lockdown and beyond…

W0081939

OMAR KURDI

ISBN 978-1-66784-292-9 (print)
ISBN 978-1-66784-293-6 (eBook)

Dear readers,

You may be here after reading my first collection "Delirium." You may be here because you like me and want to support me. You may be here because you're interested in some raw thoughts and poetry.

The writings in this collection are about divinity, love, family, parenthood, loss, and longing. My writing is raw, poorly formatted, but it's true. The writings in this collection are inspired by true events that occurred to me or people I know. My truth is in this book. Their truth is in this book. I found it, they found it and you could find it too.

"Pandemic! The Delirious Variant" is a collection of stories, thoughts and poems written during lockdown and beyond. Some pieces have music titles attached next to them. These were the music pieces I was listening to while writing that exact title. Enjoy this immersive and infectious experience.

I dedicate this book to my father Yasin Kurdi who left this world in 2018. I dedicate this book to my family and friends. Your support means the world. I want to thank the gift of music for offering an inspiration and an escape to me.

Welcome to my forever delirious mind.

Omar

Pandemic Diaries – Schindler's List by John Williams

My heart is heavy
Twenty-Twenty was too much
A pandemic
Masks not hiding enough
And racism so systemic
My heart is heavy...
People are dying
Kneeling, the peaceful protest
Became the murder weapon
Bullets are logging out lives
Love is nowhere to be found
It only comes with a receipt
So, what is it about this world?
That we can't comprehend it
We can't survive it
We can't navigate it
Without pain...hurt...tears...and expensive funerals...
And now, it's twenty twenty-one...
All I want to do is run. But how?
When I must face the sun
And what do I tell her?
That I am tired
I want to give up
How will I face the moon?
That once shielded me
What do I say to the clouds?
They saw everything unfold
What is this story to be told?
Once, lived a man
He wanted to change the world
Traveled between borders
And drafted these words
Once, lived a man
He dreamed of a peaceful land
He strived and thrived
To be strong and take a stand
Once, lived a man...A nomad in a time of uncertainty
Once, lived a man
A fighter in twenty-twenty...
A believer in twenty Twenty-One...
A human in a mad world...

Affirmations

I am worthy.

Apology – For Cersei by Ramin Djawadi

It was them
Their words
Their desires
And their scenarios
For how my life should be lived
It wasn't me...I didn't do this...
Why would a star abandon its moon?
Why would an ocean dry itself out?
You were the air I breathed...
The dreams I saw when I was awake
The laughs I never laughed
The heart that met mine halfway
The embrace that erased the world
and painted a new one just for me...
You were the light at the end of that tunnel
But now, my tunnel just grew longer
And it wasn't me...It was them...
Sorry will never be enough
For the time...The love...
The warmth you felt with me
And the security that I felt with you
We come from two different worlds
I thought we would become one
But they always saw us as two
And two we have become
Today, I'm an overthrown prince
A royal without a crown
Homeless in my own home
Alone but with my people
A coward in my eyes before yours
A hero to them
No one to you
Sorry!
I can never say it enough...

Affirmations

I deserve love.

Yasin I – The Father Main Theme by Ludovico Einaudi

I wish I had more time
More minutes
More seconds
To tell you how much I love you, dad
What is it about us?
About this culture that we belong to
That makes love a weakness
And coldness a strength
I don't want to live like this
But it's too late now
You're gone
And I'm here
Remembering every moment
Every hour that passed
Without me telling you that I love you
And without me realizing that you always loved me too

Affirmations

It is okay not to be okay.

A Validation – Crater by Justin Hurwitz

We are not perfect. Part of being human is acknowledging our faults and admitting that certain things need to be fixed. It might take us a day and it might us a year to fix these issues, but what matters is that we're on that journey of fixing. We shouldn't wait for others to fix our problems because it's never the same. Listen to your loved ones' advice but always remember, your journey of healing and fixing is to be designed by you. No one will take that journey for you. Those who love you will always understand if you're acting different, overreacting, being quiet, being too loud, being distant, or wanting to be too close. Those who love you will allow you the distance and will allow you to be close. But remember, everyone has a capacity too. Love alone is not enough. Humans have capacities. God does not. God will contain us, love us, protect us, and heal us to no limits. May your healing be quick, and may it happen as soon as you need it. We all have a different clock, and your healing is only yours, so do not worry about the timing. Trust the process and the creator of the process. Love the people around you. Love yourself.

Affirmations

I will be happy.

Tomorrow – The Wonder of Tomorrow by Alexandre Desplat

I fear for tomorrow
And I fear it
What if I wake up dead?
But feel like I'm still here
Stuck in a body that I mistreated
Trying to scream
Hoping to get someone's attention
They're listening though
To the coroner
To the funeral planner
They are with me
Praying for my unknown sins
Weeping my loss
But I am still screaming
I am fighting to open my eyes
I am exhausted
......
I can feel that white sheet wrapping me tight
I smell the musk
They say my new home is ready
You know I never thought I'd make it there
I also knew I wouldn't live forever
I don't know why but I am bothered here
This casket is small and shaky
I wonder who's carrying me now
Are they really upset?
Do they really miss me?
Some questions on my mind before I meet with God
I was waiting for this moment
Not death!
But my appointment with my creator
I have questions and I'm sure he has too
I want to know if I did well
I want to see if my stay in here will be long
Or is heaven really waiting for me?
Too many doubts
But why today?

Affirmations

It is okay to worry, but never okay to give up.

For you – The Lonely Shepherd by Hauser

I miss you
I miss your jokes
I miss your smile
I miss your laugh
I miss your whole being
And mine is not whole without you
I don't know why we can't be together
Or maybe I do…
It's forbidden.
Banned.
Maybe illegal even.
But what do I do with my heart?
It wants you
It wants only you
My heart still beats
But it no longer dances
My brain still thinks
But it no longer wanders
You took all that away with you
My heart is probably dancing around you
My brain is probably roaming near you
And me...I am not myself.
I miss you.
I miss driving to see you
I miss our dinner dates
I miss watching fireworks with you
I miss you so much
And I miss me when I was with you.

Affirmations

I must love myself to give love.

Immigrant I – Mawtini by Andrew Soueid

My heart understands pain
The pain of mourning, praying, and longing to a place
My heart belongs to too many places
I am from here and there
My free mind is Lebanese
My free will is Palestinian
My heart is Kurdish
My soul is Jordanian
And my whole being is Arab
But my experience is American
I have known too many homes
And I have chosen one of all
I have chosen to be foreign
A heartbeat for there and a heartbeat for here
I have chosen to be an immigrant
Too foreign for here and too foreign for there
…
My mission was to forever wander
To eventually settle in a place that I could call a watan
"home"
But today…my homes are many, and a place where I feel
love is mawtini *"homeland"*

Affirmations

I am foreign, and it makes me unique.

Title 8 – Song from a Secret Garden by Hauser

I see you
After every song
It's like this radio knows me
And it knows that I miss you
It plays the tunes we once danced to
And I end up gazing…waiting...for you to appear

Affirmations

I will remember the good things for the sake of my mental wellbeing.

Title 9

You're either being pushed forward, stalled, or pulled down. You should still love those who are stalling you or pulling you down the same, but don't spend much time around that energy. Not everyone wants to see you better than them, and if you're better, they'll find something to accuse you or target you with. Keep doing you. Do not delay your growth. Do not stop improving. Surround yourself with inspiration. Vibe with positivity.

Affirmations

I will work hard to achieve what I am meant to achieve.

Congratulations – Your Hands are Cold by Dario Marianelli

I can never say sorry enough
For missing out on your special day
But how could I?
Be there
Watch you hold someone else's hand
While my hands applaud
And my eyes foresee a life that I could have had with you
How could I?
Dance and celebrate
A love that you claim you want
When I know I'm all that you want?
How could I?
Sing and lend you my voice
When all I want to do is scream
And break through all that noise
To tell the world that you're mine
That my hands held yours first
That my eyes loved you first
That my heart was your home once
How could I?
Ignore my feelings and stand there to congratulate you
I couldn't.

Affirmations

I will never settle for less than what I deserve.

My Song – A Knight of the Seven Kingdoms by Ramin Djawadi

I've found you in the fog
It was clear despite the blur
You were there, and I saw you with your arms open
Ready to receive me and to comfort me
I am an impious child
I want it all, and I want it now
You took me under your wings and smiled
You gave me strength when they gave me stares
I am a distracted soul
I want to be everywhere at anytime
You breathed me into a comfortable silence
You channeled me through a blissful melody
These rhymes still linger in my memories
And I sing to myself whenever I need you
I came to you with so much fear
I knew I wanted to be here
So do what you normally do
Fix me, help me heal…Allow my heart to feel.
Your magic is what I need
…
I sing to myself every night
Hoping this song could make it right
But my tunes have been off track
And my talent is on a long pause
I don't know if it's the distance
Or if I am just not as strong
Do I miss you? Yes, I do…
And me moving on does not change that
…
This new song is not meant to be ominous
I am just trying to hymn about something precious
And if my voice does not help me, maybe my words can
And for you, letters align with the stars
Words dance to the soundtracks of life
Melodies are composed to the waves of your longing
So, I am singing to myself tonight, and every night
You're still there…
…
But I cannot lose myself too
This song is mine

Affirmations

I love myself even when it feels like I should not.

Becoming – I am Hers, She is Mine by Ramin Djawadi

You know
It was just a dream
Of self-fulfillment and love
I may have pictured that with you
But it was really me trying to love me
I'm sorry I dragged you in my mess
I hope it doesn't make you love me less
I'm torn between a self and another self
I'm broken like an unvisited dusty shelf
My books have been unopened
My corners have been forgotten
So, forgive me for using you
And I really loved you
I loved the idea of a shining star
And the mornings with a beautiful sun
I dreamed of a partner in life's thrills
And a driver when I have so many drinks
But the truth is I was just trying to find me
And with you, I really did…
And with you, I am now me…

Affirmations

I will love myself even when it feels like I should not.

Title 13 – Run by Ludovico Einaudi

Torn between the good and bad
Unsure about this path I've chosen
I want to run and never look back
But I can't leave my loved ones broken
These lies I'm lying are putting a weight
That my shoulders can no longer carry
I can't give in to a life tainted with worry
Souls like mine are meant to fly
To live, shine, travel the worlds and the seven skies
A decision must be made
The truth…
Elope
Or stay and lie even more
My brain can't take this mess anymore
Hiding between words and reactions I hate to make

Affirmations

I will make decisions that will protect my mental health first.

Title 14

My dream is an embrace
Where I'm held
Contained, loved, and protected…
My dream is a garden
Where I can grow
My dream is you

Affirmations

I will never stop dreaming.

Message to the World – Conquest of Paradise by Vangelis

These walls I live behind
They don't tell my story
The ceiling above me does not define my life
The glass windows do not always reflect reality
My life is never yours to analyze
My life is never yours to judge
My life is never yours to observe
My life is mine to live and love
My life is mine to experience
What you see is not what truth looks like
The truth can be uglier
These live scenes are not staged for your applause
The bow downs, the standing ovations, and the grand finale
are not yours
It can all be known with a question
A question that I do not have to answer
My story does not pertain to yours
My drama is not yours to discuss
What goes behind closed doors goes beyond what you may
fathom
Breathe! Let it sink in
You have no room to talk…Your options are simple
You may ask, or you may choose to walk
Whether behind me, next to me, or in front of me
My walk is mine, and yours belongs to you
A good word can do wonders
A supportive stance could mean the world
Do not assume
Do not let thoughts take over your curious mind
To each his own
And my own is as bad as it could be
But you may see good, better or worse
It is still mine, and not yours
Respect what is mine and yours
So, I can respect what is yours and mine
So, I can deal with what is mine
…
Let me break these walls
Fly through these ceilings
And shatter those windows that imprisoned my soul
Let me do it without your assumption

Affirmations

I will always live my truth.

Title 16 – Heart Shaped Box by Ramin Djawadi

The things that we do
The tears we shed for a word
All these nights you spend alone
All these fears that they're truly gone
When we stay up late to think and wonder
When we drive up there to see their window
When we walk the street searching for their shadows
When we cry… When we hope…
When we smile when we hear their names
When we write letters, they won't read…
When we wear clothes, they won't notice…
When we buy their favorite things
When we sing the melodies that they like
When we do ourselves crazy
That's when we're mad
When all we discuss is their lives
When all we look up is how our signs match
When all we dream about is the perfect date
When all we have is a ceiling to talk to
When only four walls know our secrets
When journals hide our feelings
Oh, the things that we do for love!

Affirmations

If my love is healing, I shall give it to those who need it.

Title 17

Closures matter. Good words matter. Positive notes matter. Love matters. Nothing is meant to be always closured, good, positive, or to be done with love. Nothing is always meant to be what we want it to be. The wind might go against our tides, and we must try to keep going.

If life was perfect, it'll lose its purpose. If life was perfect, we won't have a reason to work, to be happy, be sad, be thankful, or be living. Love your struggles while they shape the better version of YOU. Accept your struggles while they help you evolve. You're strong. You're unique. You're special. We're not meant to be all the same. Being different is not bad. Being generic is bad. Don't settle for the normal and set your wildness free. Life is yours to enjoy and not for others to dictate.

Smile. Cry. Fight. Love. Respect. Accept. Enjoy. Just be you while doing all that. Never give up. You'll find love within your own struggles. Love yourself to be loved. Do for yourself for others to do for you. Be you.

Affirmations

I will move on. I am built to stand up and move on.

Title 18 – La Dispute by Yann Tiersen

You put your trust in someone
You pour your heart
You give the world
And all you want in return are words
Company…Fellowship...
But all you get is being ignored
Going unnoticed…
This is your sign to walk away
Don't ever stall
Don't ever wait
The time might not be right
But those who care will always come around

Affirmations

I will trust myself first.

Title 19 – Yasak Ask by Toygar Isikli

I did love you
But I think I got scared
They call it cold feet
But I think I had lost my feet then
I lost the ability to move
I was struck by your love
And the idea that I might let you down
I…I became a coward
A character that I didn't plan to play
And I lost you along the way

Affirmations

I am okay with losing everything but losing myself.

Memories – A Life So Changed by James Horner

Do you remember
The day I saw your face
It was summer
And that was my happiest day
When my eyes saw your eyes
When you smiled and I died inside
When I knew I loved you then…?
And wanted to be with you

All I do is remember
Since the day you left me here
All those memories they hurt me
I'm living in so much fear
I thought we were stronger
And that our story wound last forever
But who knew I loved a murderer?
A criminal that killed the love in me…

Do you remember
How I begged for you to stay
And how you disappeared
And I learned to be brave
Yes, I loved you, but I love me
And your story doesn't end mine
Maybe my love was stolen forever
But I got my life to live
Without you…Without your pain…Without your hurt

Do you remember
My smile when I saw you gone
Did you expect me to cry?
Oh no I'm not that one
I got strength in me
More than you could imagine

Affirmations

I will remember you for the good memories, and I thank you for the bad ones. I now know myself a little better because of you.

Yasin II – To My Father by Guy Manoukian

I've chosen a new home for me
Somewhere in a wild, wild place…
You know, I've always imagined my home to be white
But with so many colors inside
And a stairwell to a heavenly upstairs
There, you'll find the California
And you'll find me in an imagined placenta
Wondering if it's time to be reborn
Or time to die inside
This home I've chosen
Has so many cells, with so many broken walls
And it has a grand ballroom for my memories to waltz
And dance away the events of that unspoken of day
The day the sun rose with one ray less
The day the clouds watched over me as I cried
As I mourned, and wished that my tears were just washing
off my sins
And not bidding farewell to a man with none
See, I've chosen a new home, dad…
A home where your picture continues to inspire
A home where your voice can still be heard
A home where you are still there
And I am there too waiting for a scolding
I've a chosen a haven away from a reality nightmare
A treehouse with a one-way ladder
And a memory box that I will never leave locked
I've a chosen a home far from my quiet room
Far from this cold hallway waiting for the ringing of your
oxygen machine
Distant from the memory of you grasping a breath to live
I've chosen a home where I can miss you without missing
you
Where I am not a jailed grieving man
Where I am with you all the time

Affirmations

I will never forget the lessons my parents taught me. Number one lesson: watch your tongue. If you protect it, it will protect you. If you betray it, it will betray you.

Title 22 – Ucurumdun Sen by Toygar Isikli

Dance in the corners of my sorrow
Sway with the rhythm of my pain
And tell me if you still love me
Will we have a tomorrow
Or is this my new destiny
I was born without a backbone
I was born without a base
And you were the one and only
The royal to my throne
And the destination of my chase
Does my hurting make you happy?
Or do my tears fulfill your thirst?
Tell me so I can hurt even more
And never allow my bubble to burst
Is this the kingdom you've imagined
And is this how you learned to rule
To leave me begging for mercy
And watch me dance like a fool
Dance along my chaotic misery
Travel with me through this muddle
Dance in the cages inside me
While I dance in a different puzzle
Let me be your prime performance
And you can be my only audience
Dance like you've never danced before
I was born to watch you dance

Affirmations

I will never dance to a song that I don't like.

Awakening – Bathroom Dance by Hildur Guonadottir

It could take me hours and sometimes days
But in the end, I know…It comes to me…
I wake up after a long sleep
The dreams I once saw
Return to me in daylight
The haunting sounds of darkness
Become my ringing alarm
What I feared to once see
Turns into my favorite sight

They bet on my forever coma
That I'll never open my eyes
I hear them whisper about it
As my voice leaves me and flies
To reach my friends in another world
Where my words matter
Where I don't stutter
This ill man in his death bed is now awake
He realized what is really at stake
His life…His passion…His voice
His hunger for something better
His tears now water his ambition
His drive no longer needs an ignition

You are not allowed to use me anymore
My heart is no longer yours
My embrace can't hold you
My arms will reach out to something larger
No human is worthy of this thriving soul
My dreams are no longer yours
My eyes no longer see you
They see something better and farther
….
They see me

Affirmations

I will not be taken advantage of.

Title 24 – Konaktaki Yalnizlik by Toygar Isikli

You walked by me and stopped
I could feel your racing heartbeats
They were marching towards an unknown
You saw me
I saw you
I felt you
But you did not
I am not a statue
I am not in a museum
This life is more than an exhibition
I am more than an attraction
Walk by me again
Feel my pain
Touch my heart
Help me escape this confinement

Affirmations

I will not be a prisoner of my thoughts, or anyone else's.

Yasin III – The Second Meeting by Omar Khairat

So often we leave places early, end conversations early, and just feel rushed at everything we do. There are times when we feel like there are things that we need to say but can't. There are things we need to do but we can't. Trips we need to make, conversations we need to have, jobs we need to leave, jobs we need to accept, situations we need to adapt to, and losses we need to deal with. Life is all of that, but also a little more than that. Life is not for early departures, short conversations, and missed trips. Life is for experiences. Life is for those moments when you decided to stay a little longer. Life is when a planned ten-minute conversation extends to hours. Life is when an unplanned trip happens to a place that you never thought of. Life is for the good and bad. The bad can always turn into good, and vice versa. It's our choice. It's in our control. Our thought system controls how we absorb and react to things. We have all dealt with happy moments, and we have all experienced a loss of any kind at some point. We can survive both if we understand that these moments are our own to deal with. Advice works, but it's our story to write. It's your ink that's writing it, not someone else's so why waste it. Listen to your heart, listen to your mind, and allow yourself to absorb things before you react. I know it sounds platonic, but as my dad's four years is approaching, all I could think of is how I've been dealing with this. I haven't listened to a single advice given to me. I just swam through the waves and navigated through the struggles as they came in my face. The life jacket that someone might throw to save me could work, but a life isn't saved by just living.

Affirmations

I will be there for myself as much as I will be there for anyone else who needs me.

Yasin IV – Breathless by Zade Dirani

Nothing is more intriguing to me like reading stories of people losing one of their parents. It puts tears in my eyes. It reminds me that we take our parents for granted. It reminds me that life is not guaranteed. We make mistakes as sons and daughters, and parents can make mistakes too. The goal is to raise good kids. The goal is to please our parents with good work. The goal is to fulfill our dreams, and the dreams our parents are dreaming through us. There's a story that I will never forget though. An old friend that lost his father and lost his mother five years after when he was 16. I cried. We all cried. He grew up to be a very successful individual making his parents proud wherever they are. Don't take your parents for granted. We will never be able to handle their loss. I listen to how my father speaks of his mother that passed away before I got to meet her. I listen to how my mother speaks of her father that I loved so much. I see how much pain they hide when telling these stories and hope to never go through this pain. I think to myself; I wish I could go before they would go, but then I remember that they wouldn't be able to handle it, and it's unfair to make such a wish. I just want to take this moment to thank the Lord for blessing me with good parents despite all the ups and downs that are normal in any parent-children's relationships. Go tell your parents that you love them. Go tell your kids that you love them. Make memories and don't just spend time together. I wish I had more time to tell my dad that I love him.

Affirmations

I will love my parents. I will give them a better love than they have given me.

Immigrant II – Inta Omri Tribute by Michel Fadel

My homes are many. As an Arab, my pain transcends from the Atlantic Ocean to the Gulf. As an Arab, I learned to watch the news every day to make sure the places and people I love are okay. As an Arab, I mastered the art of praying for turmoil to end and mastered the art of being numb after seeing so much destruction happening in the places that I love. My whole being is an Arab, and today, I am in pain. The numbers of those who are hurt keep on growing. The smokes are reaching new heights. The blood of the innocent is watering our grounds. The sounds of explosions have become our goodnight lullabies. The images of broken things that we used to see on the web, are what we see on the ground. My whole being is an Arab, and this Arab is tired. We need a miracle. We need to pray a little harder. But most importantly, we need to stand our ground a bit stronger, scream a little louder, and make our demands heard. My whole being is Arab, and this Arab is in pain. Pain for the world. Pain for my so many homes that are bleeding, breaking down, and trying to rise again. And they will rise. My whole being is Arab, and all we know is to fight to survive. We will survive.

Affirmations

I will represent my heritage loud and proud.

Title 28 – Kalimat by Duo Aznem

We are humans. We make mistakes. We fall. We rise. We are made to navigate through hardships. We also have the blessing of choosing the right people to be with us as we swim through the waves. But we make wrong choices sometimes. We follow the wrong leads. We trust the wrong people. We hold on to things that will only hurt us. We are humans, so it's okay, these things can happen. What can't happen is staying still, allowing someone to stall you, and pouring your heart to those who only know how to shatter it. Don't hate these people. Love them. Pray for them. Allow them some time to grow, but away from you. They will eventually find their way to you when they're ready. Only then, your relationship with them will become healthier. Don't be upset if they never find your way to you. Continue to pray for them. It was just never meant to be.

Affirmations

My mistakes will not break me.

Title 29 – Soupir Eternil by Dhafer Youssef

Religions are labels. What matters is someone's faith. Faith leads you to being a good person. Following a label for the "follow" won't do you any good. I may be Muslim by label, but I am a follower of God, I believe in all the messengers, I believe in love, respect, and I believe in being a good person. I am not a preacher, and no one's knowledge will ever be enough to just preach. We lose so much love when we focus on the technical aspects of faith rather than loving God, his people, and being genuinely good to each other. God belongs to humanity and not to a specific religion. God created us all with the same amount of love, so who are we to hate others just because they worship differently. Faith without love has a weak foundation. Start your day with loving your creator, loving what he created, and loving yourself. That's faith. Everything else falls in place once your heart finds the love it needs.

Affirmations

My faith is for me. Your faith is for you. I owe you love and respect, as much as you owe me love and respect.

Title 30 – Any Other Name by Thomas Newman

What you see from the outside may be true, but it is not your place to judge it. What may need a fixing, can be done quietly. Hearts can be comforted with kind words. Minds can be rested with comforting hugs. Lives can be saved without a spotlight. Take a step back and let it come to you. Things are more beautiful in silence.

Affirmations

My truth is beautiful even if it does not appeal to others.

Title 31 – Don't Lose Your Mind by Omar Khairat

Get up…look in the mirror and stare for a bit. Get up and speak to yourself. Ask yourself questions. Try to remember the good things and the bad things. Wake up! Life is still yours…Life is still yours to live, to enjoy, explore, and experience…You fell in love? You lost a friend? You lost a loved one? You failed a test? Whatever happened to you, someone else is going through something worse. Get up and feel blessed that you are still breathing, you have a place to stay in, a meal to eat, and someone to talk to. Get up! Don't settle for the loss whatever it is…We all lose, but we all could win…Pick the right fight and go for it…You are not a loser; you are not a griever...Be thankful…Go say thank you to those who have hurt you, to those who have failed you, who underestimated you, and who tried to demean you…Get up and prove yourself wrong. Get up!

Affirmations

Every day is a new day, and I will treat every day differently.

Yasin V – Farewell Child by Adel Hakki

My happiness is in half
My hope is in half
My life is half a life
But my sadness…My sadness is whole…
Because when I remember you, halves disappear…

Affirmations

I will allow myself to grief, but I will not let it control the way I live.

Title 33 – Careless Whisper by Hauser

Do you laugh at my funny jokes?
Or is it just to make me feel good about myself
You don't have to laugh to make me happy
Your presence is happiness
I see the world in your eyes
And in your eyes, I see my world
I love the life in you, and with you I want to live
I am a wanderer in your land
I am an explorer in your continents
You are the only map I need
You are the only compass I follow
So now that I have told you what you are to me
Do you really laugh?
Is it from the heart or out of pity?
Do you see me the way I see you?
Too many questions…I know.
I just need an answer to one
Where do I stand with you?

Affirmations

I will not wait for someone's validation.

Title 34 – Jake's First Flight by James Horner

Accepting that you can make mistakes is the first step to becoming a better person. Mistakes are a must to improve yourself. It doesn't matter how many times you do things wrong if you eventually do it right. Bear with yourself in this journey of discovery. No one said discovering your purpose in life was easy. Be positive, be humble, be respectful, and be accepting. It's okay if you feel weak. It's okay if you lose track sometimes. What's not okay is to accept defeat and being out of track. Go ahead & find your way. Life is yours to discover.

Affirmations

I will always be content with what I have, but I will never stop exploring for more.

Title 35 – Rose Theme by James Horner

Think of me as a rose
A gift from a massive garden
You water me every morning
You watch me dance with the wind
And I am always there for you to smell

Think of me as a picture
A memory from an eventful life
You hang me in a specific corner
You look at me when you walk in the door
And I am always there to greet you

Think of me as anything
Let me be your something
Make me what you want to make me
Love me the way you want to love me
I will always be there waiting for you

Think of me as a forest
A jungle of your tangled emotions
You come to me whenever things fall apart
You lay on my branches when you're down
And I will always be there to support you

Affirmations

I will allow my imagination to just be.

Title 36 – Adagio by Hauser

Leave…
Take whatever you still own of me and go
I will learn to live without these pieces
I will practice breathing a different air
I will adjust to not missing you
I will get to know myself
Leave!
And do not come back.

Affirmations

I will not accept hurt from someone just because I love them.

Title 37 – My Story by Khaled Hammad

I wasn't myself that night
I was high on loving you
On a different cloud colored with your laughter
And scented with your warm embrace
I did what I shouldn't have done
I'm sorry for that
But I can never apologize for how I feel
It feels right to spend my lifetime apologizing
And trying to remind you that I am crazy about you
I'm sorry…
Sorry for my misjudgment
Sorry for my wrongdoing
Sorry for making you cry
But never sorry for loving you
Never sorry for wanting to spend my lifetime with you
I'll climb the tallest mountain
And swim the deepest sea
Travel to a different horizon
To tell you of who I ought to be
To be a friend
To be a confidant
To be a lover…a hero…
And a warrior in this fight for you
So, accept me as a martyr
Celebrate me as a soldier
Stab me with my own sword
Do what you desire
Let me apologize
Let me repent
If it keeps me with you

Affirmations

I will own up to my mistakes. I will learn how to become a better person.

Questions – Come Back by Dario Marianelli

Tell me if it's true
Did your plans go through?
With your new lover
What did you two do
To stay together
Unlike me and you
Tell me
What did I do wrong?
When were my feelings short?
And why wasn't I enough?
Tell me
Are you happier now?
That you're in his arms
And not in mine
Are you safer?
In his haven
And not in my mess
Tell me
Do I get a second chance?
Or is it over?
Tell me
So, I can tell him
To love you, and care for you
To protect you, and live through you
To never leave you
So, you don't ask him all these questions
So, you don't ask him to tell you

Affirmations

I deserve the truth.

Title 38

I can't stay close
I won't go far
You're an overdose
Numbness to my scar
They say it's time to go
But I can't just leave
I have love for you
A longing for your heart
And maybe I should go
But before I do
Please remember
My love was whole
My heart was yours
I had to choose between life alone
Or death with you
I want to live.

Affirmations

My sanity is more important than anything else that gives me temporary pleasure.

Immigrant III – The Godfather Theme by 2 Cellos

I am shattered and confused
I am from so many places
I am homeless in my eyes
And with a home in yours
I am happy and I'm sad
And I'm close and I'm far
Here I have you
But my lover and I are apart
This is not easy
I need to figure this out
I feel so torn
And haunted with doubts
Do I have to stay here?
Or can I just go back
Will I have a better life there
Or is it better to let go and stay
It's getting crazy
I'm missing my old life
But I like it here too
I'm embarking on something new
Can I have two homes
One for me and one for me
With memories from each place
And friends that equally love me
Can I belong to here and there?
And be loyal to it all

Affirmations

I will be loyal to the things, people, and places that ignite positivity in me.

Title 40 – Briony by Dario Marianelli

How can I live knowing you're not mine?
Is this a life that I really want for me
To sleep and wake up with you on my mind
For your face to be what I need to see
I really love you
More than I should for my own good
I really need you
And I feel like I'm always stuck
I am torn between saying something or nothing
If only the skies can guide me
If only you can just contain me
The words will just come out

Affirmations

I will never conform to what society wants me to look like.

Christine's Growth – Runaway by Ramin Djawadi

You talk to him
He seems like a hopeless case
And you remind him that one day
He will lose you
You finish your conversation
With so much confusion
He leaves you to cry
You are not deceived
This is true
He never made you feel close
He never gave you a reason
And every time a confrontation happens
You learn something
Every argument leads to an awakening
And when you decide to move on
A branch of you will break
To allow another one to grow

Affirmations

I will grow out of every negative situation.

Yasin VI – Without You by Alexandre Desplat

Years have passed
And I now understand
I figured the game out & mastered it
I love it now after living in its mazes
I know now why God created me
And the purpose of this life I didn't live
I'm alive and I have a soul
And I am dead
My soul decorated my scars
But I survived
I made a life out of a death
And found an oasis within my pain…
I escaped with myself to the sky
I spoke to the creator and complained
I told him that I was ready to die
If this was really my destiny
And I went back to my world waiting for destiny's answer
And then people colored my life
And I loved everything in its everything
My sadness disappeared within the corners of my heart
My smile defeated my hurting
And then I understood
And then I knew
That I was created to smile
That we were created to be happy
To dance through our pain and forget
We were created strong…
I now understand
That my sorrow won't bring you back
And missing you is my sacred right
And that my smile won
And my sadness is still there
But applauding

Affirmations

I will never allow my sadness to come in the way of remembering the good memories of those who left.

To My Palestinian Grandmother – Mawtini by Andre Soueid

I am not Palestinian, but my grandmother is
I am not Palestinian, but my friends are
I am everything but Palestinian
-
Omar, I was 13 years old then
I had dreams and hopes
I had friends, Christians, and Jews
I lost these dreams and hopes
They walked into my door
My mom was thrown on the floor
My dad rushed to get us out
We were kicked out
We were removed, banned,
My dreams were demolished
Son, Palestine was gone
My grandmother cried
And I died a little inside
I am not Palestinian
But my grandmother is
I am not Palestinian
But my friends are
They were raised in palaces so far
Places they were forced to call home
Homes with no flying drones
Yet their relatives still there
In A Palestine they once shared
But today, that Palestine is occupied
It's barricaded, blocked, caged
Their bodies are caged
But Palestinian souls are free
They were like a never dying tree
Branches grow, roots remain, leaves fall
But new ones prevail
I am not Palestinian
But it's like I am
I am not Palestinian
But I never needed to be one
Palestinian is not a nationality
Palestinian is an identity
Palestine is a passion, an emotion

A Resurrection of love and hope
Palestine is resistance
Palestine is love
I am not Palestinian
I am human
Palestine is my cause
I am not Palestinian
But I often sing to Palestine
Will I See you; will I see you?
Safely comforted and victoriously honored
Will I see you
In your eminence reaching to the stars
My Homeland…
I am not Palestinian
But what am I?
I looked in the mirror
I smiled, and I broke it.
Why did I break it?
Because I can never be a Palestinian
I am not as strong…

Affirmations

I will always give solidarity to those who are oppressed no matter who they are, where they are, or what they look like.

Title 44 – Bring Me to Life by Evanescence

As my heart tries to heal
Thunder strikes for a surprise
It takes everything so I no longer feel
And it leaves me with thoughts that I despise
My soul can no longer handle such pain
My being is tired
My mind is stained
I am not me anymore
The universe closed every door
I am drowning in a sea of false hopes
I am hanging onto loose ropes
I am not myself.
My smiles are half smiles
My happiness is not whole
Is this a call for help?
Maybe.
Is this a poem?
Maybe.
Am I okay?
Maybe. Maybe not.

Affirmations

I will ask for help when I need it.

Victory – A Lannister Always Pays his Debts by Ramin Djawadi

There's nothing left to say
My screams are quiet
I finally beat this trident
I finally eloped far away
After my hands were tied
I danced…
I moved to the sound of my hurting
My arms swayed as I mourned you
We sang for your farewell
You tapped your feet on the ground
Stomped like a fallen soldier
You left this battle alone
As I stayed behind and cried
But my tears dried up
To celebrate my freedom
I wept but I prevailed
I won and you failed
…
I planted this desert
After I buried your memory in it
Roses grew over your dirt
And they smell like victory

Affirmations

I will celebrate all my victories, whether big or small. A win is a win.

The End – Now We Are Free by Hauser

Imagine being born into a world that you feel is small to hold you. Imagine being born into a life that you live just to live. I am this human who sometimes feels like the world is not big enough, and that life is still not being lived. I have lived so many years holding so much in. I have lived through so many moments where I wish I had said something but did not. This book is for every moment I wished I had said something but did not. This book is for everyone who felt the need to speak up but could not. Every piece in this book was written after a certain event that has occurred. Stories about love, parenthood, family, relationships, and swimming through the sea we call life. This book is inspired by true events that occurred to me or people I have come to know in my 31 years of life. You might think after reading this book that I have come to know many interesting people. You are thinking right. Every person whether I've known for a day or for 20 years has helped shape the person that I am today. Every story has affected these pieces in this book. Every piece in this book represents a piece of humanity. Every piece in this book is something that was meant to be said but was not. You will notice a lot of repeated words, and they represent a reality we are all searching for.

Thank you for reading my pandemic thoughts. You are now officially infected with the Delirious Variant.

With love, gratitude, and thanks,

Omar